W9-AXK-302

WILD ABOUT SNAKES

COBRAS

BY MEGAN KOPP

Consultant:
Robert Mason, PhD
Professor of Zoology
J.C. Braly Curator of Vertebrates
Oregon State University, Corvallis

CAPSTONE PRESS
a capstone imprint

Edge Books are published by Capstone Press,
151 Good Counsel Drive, P.O. Box 669, Mankato, Minnesota 56002.
www.capstonepub.com

Books published by Capstone Press are manufactured with paper
containing at least 10 percent post-consumer waste.

Library of Congress Cataloging-in-Publication Data
Kopp, Megan.
    Cobras / by Megan Kopp.
    p. cm.—(Edge books. Wild about snakes)
    Includes bibliographical references and index.
    Summary: "Describes cobras, including their distinctive characteristics,
habitats, and defenses"—Provided by publisher.
    ISBN 978-1-4296-5430-2 (library binding)
    ISBN 978-1-4296-6256-7 (paperback)
    1. Cobras—Juvenile literature. I. Title.
QL666.O64K67 2011
597.96'42—dc22   2010027376

Editorial Credits
Kathryn Clay and Anthony Wacholtz, editors; Kyle Grenz, designer; Eric Gohl,
    media researcher; Eric Manske, production specialist

TABLE OF CONTENTS

CHARMING COBRAS

Swaying in time to the tune of the flute, a cobra rises out of the basket. Its trademark hood is raised, and a crowd gathers to watch the charmer and his snake. It looks like this deadly **reptile** is under a spell, but don't be fooled.

In ancient times, having power over snakes was considered a magical gift. But it's not magic, just knowledge of snake behavior. Cobras don't have ears, and they can't hear the high notes of a flute. The snake is really following the movement of the instrument from side to side.

Snake charmers typically use cobras because the snakes flatten their neck ribs when threatened. Doing this pulls the skin into a hood. Cobras also raise their bodies upright to get a better view. But these "dancing" snakes pose a great danger. Cobras are filled with **venom**. One strike may kill the charmer. It's all part of the thrill of watching a charmer and his snake.

reptile—a cold-blooded animal that breathes air and has a backbone; most reptiles lay eggs and have scaly skin

venom—a poisonous substance produced by some snakes

5

Deadly Bites

With their upper bodies raised several feet off the ground, cobras are impressive snakes. They are among the most easily recognizable snakes in the world. They are also among the deadliest. While other snakes have venom that is more toxic, cobras often inject much more poison when they bite.

Most snake bites occur in South Asia, Southeast Asia, and Sub-Sarahan Africa. India tops the list of countries with the most fatal snake bites. Each year about 35,000 people worldwide die from cobra bites.

The venom from a cobra bite acts quickly once it enters the bloodstream. Symptoms include dizziness, drowsiness, and blurred vision. In a human being, the venom can cause paralysis or death within 15 minutes of a single bite.

The Cobra Family

Cobras belong to a family of snakes called Elapidae. Elapids also include mambas, coral snakes, taipans, and kraits. All members of this family have short, hollow fangs and produce deadly venom.

A king cobra can kill an elephant with a single bite.

Cobras are usually recognized by the wide hood around their necks. The hood is formed when a snake's muscles move the rib bones in its neck. This pulls the skin out in the shape of a hood. Cobras spread out their hoods when they are bothered or feel threatened. Doing this makes the snake look larger to its enemies.

Cobras come in many different colors and sizes. Most cobras are black or brown, but some are red, orange, or yellow. Some **species**, like the cape cobra, can be one of many different colors. Cape cobras in the Kalahari Desert in South Africa are usually bright yellow. Southern cape cobras are normally dark in color. Egyptian cobras sometimes have wide stripes of brown or black that can be seen when the hood is up.

Egyptian cobras are often called asps. These are the most common cobras in Africa.

Cobras are impressive snakes when it comes to size. Growing to more than 18 feet (5.5 meters) in length, king cobras are the longest venomous snakes in the world. They weigh up to 44 pounds (20 kilograms). At 4 feet (1.2 meters) long, the ringhal is the smallest cobra. Some ringhals weigh less than 1 pound (0.5 kg).

The average height of an American male is 5 feet, 10 inches (178 centimeters).

species—a specific type of animal or plant

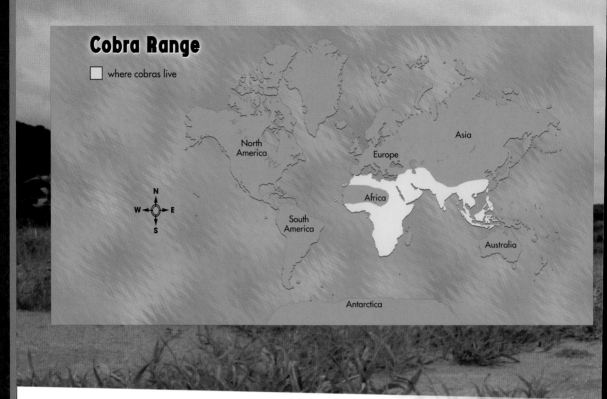

Cobra Range

☐ where cobras live

North America

Europe

Asia

Africa

South America

Australia

Antarctica

N
W—E
S

A Place to Call Home

Depending on the species, cobras' **habitats** vary greatly. They can be found in the water, on land, underground, or even in trees. They are common throughout Africa, Asia, the Middle East, and the Philippines.

In India, king cobras can be found in jungles, forests, open fields, and hilly areas. The Philippine cobra likes low-lying forests and fields near water. The Storm's water cobra spends most of its time in the water. This African cobra can stay underwater for up to 10 minutes and can dive more than 80 feet (24 m) underwater. The black desert cobra can be found in Iraq, Israel, and Jordan. This species prefers dry desert and rocky areas. The tree cobra from central Africa is an excellent climber. It spends most of its time high above the forest floor.

are also called ectotherms. "Ecto" means "outside" and "therm" means "temperature." Snake blood isn't actually cold. Snakes' bodies may become cold to match the outside temperature, but their blood never gets cold.

Warming Up

Like all reptiles, cobras are **cold-blooded**. This means that they can't control their body temperature. They rely on warm air temperatures, rocks, and water to heat their bodies. When their bodies get too cold, cobras become slow and sluggish.

Many cobras are most active at dawn and dusk when it's not too hot or too cold. Like many snakes, cobras lay in the sun to warm up. When they get too warm, cobras find a shady place to rest.

cold-blooded—having a body temperature that changes with the surroundings

Finding Food

Depending on the size of their last meal, cobras can go for days or weeks without eating. But when they do eat, cobras like big meals. Most cobras eat a variety of **prey**. Frogs, fish, lizards, and birds are all part of a cobra's diet. A cobra may also eat small mammals and other snakes.

Hungry cobras move out of their resting places to search for food. Cobras smell prey using their forked tongues. A cobra flicks its tongue in and out to capture smells in the air and on the ground. When a cobra closes its mouth, the tongue delivers the smells to an organ located on the roof of its mouth. This area is called the Jacobson's organ. Snakes use the organ to help recognize prey.

A Killer Bite

When prey is detected, cobras attack fast. Because its fangs are small, a cobra tends to hang on tightly to its catch. The snake's jaws aren't strong enough to crush the animal. Instead, cobras chew on their prey long enough to inject their deadly venom.

Cobra venom is made up of **neurotoxins**. This venom attacks the nervous system of the prey. It affects the animal's ability to breathe and stops its heart from beating. Cobras swallow their prey whole after the venom takes effect.

The Value of Venom

While cobra venom can be deadly, it is also being used to save lives. Researchers are combining cobra venom with human proteins to make medicine. One medicine made from cobra venom helps to thin blood so it won't clot too fast. Other drugs made with venom have been created to treat arthritis, heart attacks, and strokes.

neurotoxin—a chemical substance that attacks the nervous system

17

Baby Cobras

Most cobras lay eggs. Each year they lay one **clutch**. The number of eggs in the clutch varies by species, but most clutches have 10 to 30 eggs. After laying the eggs, the mother snake covers them and slithers away. The baby snakes are able to care for themselves right out of the shell. Young cobras can even flare their hoods as soon as they hatch.

clutch–a group of eggs laid by a single female

Unlike other cobras, king cobras build nests before laying eggs. They guard the eggs until they hatch. Scientists are still trying to learn why these snakes' reproductive habits differ from other cobras.

South African ringhals give birth to 10 to 30 fully-developed baby snakes.

LIFE AND DEATH

Cobras can live up to 20 years in the wild. But in order to survive, they must learn to avoid **predators**. Tiny mongooses are one of their most dangerous predators. Mongooses are small, ferret-like mammals that eat rats, lizards, eggs, and snakes. They attack with lightning speed and grab snakes on the back of the neck. Once they have the snake in their jaws, there is no escape.

The secretary bird is another danger for cobras. Secretary birds live in Africa. These 4-foot (1.2-m) birds use their long legs to slash the back of a snake's head with razor-sharp talons.

predator—an animal that hunts other animals for food

Attacking Enemies

When a king cobra feels threatened, it flares its hood. Then it hisses in a deep growling tone like a dog. King cobras can also raise their bodies 6 feet (1.8 m) off the ground to make themselves appear larger.

More than 12 cobra species appear to spit at their enemies. Even though they are called spitting cobras, these snakes don't actually spit their venom. They spray it by squeezing muscles around their venom sacs. Doing this forces the venom out the front openings in the fangs. These snakes can spray venom up to 6.5 feet (2 meters).

As cobras spray venom, they quickly move their heads back and forth. The movement spreads the venom, which helps it hit its target. Though the spray is not deadly, it can land in the eyes and cause scarring or blindness.

Some species of cobras have developed unique strategies to avoid attacks. Egyptian and Mozambique spitting cobras go limp, let their tongues hang out of their mouths, and play dead. Predators often leave a dead cobra alone.

Chapter 4

CONTINUING DISCOVERIES

There are still more questions than answers when it comes to cobras and their survival. But scientists around the world continue to make important discoveries about these mysterious snakes.

The Central Asian cobra is a dark-colored snake. It can reach up to 5 feet (1.5 m) in length and lives throughout Asia. Until recently, scientists believed there was only one species of this snake. Studies now show that there are nearly a dozen species. Some of these newly discovered species are spitting cobras and others are not. Researchers are studying their venom and scale patterns to help separate the species.

In 2007 scientists agreed that Ashe's spitting cobra was a separate species from the black-necked spitting cobra. Both venom and scale patterns were different in the Ashe's spitting cobra. The recent discovery of this new species makes scientists wonder if there are more cobras still to be discovered.

Tracking Snakes

Following snakes is no easy task. So how do you track a serpent? Carry a big stick and wave it around in the air. The big stick is a metal antenna used to pick up signals from a radio transmitter placed in a cobra.

A scientist can use a long rod to handle a dangerous snake from a distance. The rod allows the scientist to pick up the snake without allowing it to get too close.

First researchers must catch the snakes. Then the snakes are put to sleep while veterinarians insert transmitters just under the snakes' skin. Once the transmitters are in place, the snakes are released. Researchers follow the snakes as they travel. They can tell how long a snake spends in one place and where it moves. This information helps build a map of the snake's activities. By tracking the snakes, scientists are learning how cobras move daily and as the seasons change. The more knowledge scientists have about cobras, the easier it will be for them to protect the snakes.

Snake Study

Scientists in India started the first-ever radio tracking study of a snake species. Researchers are following king cobras to understand their movement and habitats. They are also gathering information about the snakes' mating habits, diet, and growth.

Saving Snakes

There's a chance that undiscovered cobra species might be disappearing before we even know of their existence. Scientists are worried about the future of cobras. Cobras are hunted for their skins, which are used to make wallets, purses, belts, and shoes. People clearing forests and expanding cities are destroying the snakes' natural habitats. The use of pesticides is also threatening cobras' survival.

Some people wonder why we should protect such deadly creatures. Few people realize how important cobras are to the **ecosystem**. Many species of cobras feed on rats. Rats can carry diseases that could make people sick. Cobras help keep the rat population from becoming too large. Scientists have also just starting using cobra venom in drugs to help cure illnesses. If cobras disappear, so does the chance to explore cures with their venom.

Scientists are working to save cobras by creating safe habitats for the snakes. They also educate people about the benefits of cobras. The scientists encourage people to use caution and avoid killing the snakes.

ecosystem—a group of animals and plants that work together with their surroundings

GLOSSARY

clutch (KLUHCH)—a group of eggs laid by a single female

cold-blooded (KOHLD-BLUH-duhd)—having a body temperature that changes with the surroundings

ecosystem (EE-koh-sis-tuhm)—a group of animals and plants that work together with their surroundings

habitat (HAB-uh-tat)—the natural place and conditions in which a plant or animal lives

neurotoxin (nur-oh-TOK-sen)—a chemical substance that attacks the nervous system

predator (PRED-uh-tur)—an animal that hunts other animals for food

prey (PRAY)—an animal hunted by another animal for food

reptile (REP-tile)—a cold-blooded animal that breathes air and has a backbone; most reptiles lay eggs and have scaly skin

species (SPEE-sheez)—a specific type of animal or plant

talon (TAL-uhn)—a long, sharp claw

venom (VEN-uhm)—a poisonous substance produced by some snakes

READ MORE

Fiedler, Julie. *Cobras.* Scary Snakes.
New York: PowerKids Press, 2008.

Smith, Michael. *Cobras and Their Kin.*
Pittsburgh, Penn.: Dorrance Publishing, 2009.

White, Nancy. *King Cobras: The Biggest
Venomous Snakes of All!* Fangs. New York:
Bearport Publishing, 2009.

INTERNET SITES

FactHound offers a safe, fun way to find Internet
sites related to this book. All of the sites on
FactHound have been researched by our staff.

Here's all you do:

Visit *www.facthound.com*

Type in this code: 9781429654302

INDEX